GRIEF: COPING WITH HOLIDAYS

JODY NEUFELD

Energion Publications
Gonzalez, FL
2016

ISBN10: 1-63199-335-6
ISBN13: 978-1-63199-335-0

Energion Publications
P. O. Box 841
Gonzalez, FL 32560

energion.com
pubs@energion.com

TABLE OF CONTENTS

An Email from my Friend, Dr. David Alan Black, October 2016

It's weird how life works. If you had asked me a year ago what my big plans for the fall break of 2016 were, they wouldn't have included a climbing trip to Colorado. They wouldn't have included writing a book about my journey since Becky [his wife] went to heaven. They wouldn't have included starting a Greek class in Hawaii. It seems like I've packed in more fun, crazy, and incredible adventures in the past 365 days than in the previous 10 years put together. I have no doubt that the next 365 days are going to be filled with even more laughter and tears and challenges and opportunities. For starters, in just one month I'll be remembering Becky's Home Going exactly 3 years ago. How in the world have I made it this far?

Climbing a 14er [14,000 foot mountain] has become a parable for me. You walk and walk and walk. You stumble. You mope. You decide to quit. You sit on a rock, feeling totally defeated, and you almost break out into tears. Then, all of a sudden, you're at the summit. In complete disbelief you ask yourself, "How did THAT happen?"

In all honesty, the race of life in the past three years seems like a blur to me. I usually don't remember the hard parts, just as you forget the pain of the climb once you reach the top. But I WANT to remember. I want to remember the struggles, the frustrations, the times I felt like giving up — and then pushing past the pain, deciding I can finish the race by taking just one step at a time if that's what it takes until you KNOW you're going to make it no matter what.

Most importantly of all, I want to remember WHY I'm going to make it. His name is Jesus, and He's a Master Climber, and you know what? Just as He found the courage and strength to finish His race, you too will find joy and strength in the journey, and while the pain and discouragement never disappear completely, you always find a way through them.

Today I'm taking the day off from climbing. I think I just need to recharge my batteries. And spend time with the One who designed the race and completed it and now stands with open arms ready to welcome me and you and all of us across the finish line.

INTRODUCTION

Holidays aren't always jolly when you have experienced the loss of a loved one, a job, marriage, or had any number of situations involving loss. The first round of holidays after a loss are especially difficult to navigate as you attempt to find the "new normal" in the old traditions that have been changed and redirected.

My first experience with loss came when I was about five years old. My father, a truck driver, was laid off from his job and spent the next year at home caring for me while my mother took a job as a saleswoman at our local J C Penny store. My parents had a very traditional 1950's marriage and so this change in roles was very difficult for them both. As a young child, I have only "flash" memories of my father's poor cooking skills and my mother trying to work 40 hours/week and still cook dinner every night, buy the groceries, do the laundry and fall asleep before I did at night.

My next experience was at age 14 and is much more vivid. My grandfather died after falling down some stairs. He was a great story-teller and much loved by the grandchildren for those stories in which the fish got larger with each telling and local characters would often imbibe one or two beers too many! This caused them to participate in antics that my grandfather never participated in, of course, but was there only to tell the tales, much to my grandmother's dismay! Now Grandpa was gone and his stories would have to be told by another generation.

Even now, almost 50 years later, I can feel tears come to my eyes as I remember my grandfather. Why is that? Am I still grieving for him? Are tears only manifestations of sadness or are they also the mark of good memories and happier, simpler times?

I hope in this booklet you will find practical ways to walk in your grief journey *through* the holidays. I make no claim that you will find a way to avoid questions, tears and your feelings. But

I hope you will have tools to help you move along through the holidays and allow people to encourage you, and even politely put limitations on *their* expectations and needs, and think of your own needs first.

I am a Christian and could not make this journey and share what I have learned without speaking of my faith, both the strengths that lifted me and the questions with which I wrestled. All feelings, questions and discussions are welcomed and encouraged. Those that are ignored, covered up and painted over, will become wounds that fester and bring on sickness which manifest in our spirits as well as our bodies. Treatment can often involve pain but ignoring a problem does not make it go away. Those who are around us, family and friends as well as professionals, help and support us, bringing about our healing and rejuvenation.

> *All praise to God, the Father of our Lord Jesus Christ. God is our merciful Father and the source of all comfort. He comforts us in all our troubles so that we can comfort others. When they are troubled, we will be able to give them the same comfort God has given us. For the more we suffer for Christ, the more God will shower us with his comfort through Christ. Even when we are weighed down with troubles, it is for your comfort and salvation! For when we ourselves are comforted, we will certainly comfort you. Then you can patiently endure the same things we suffer. We are confident that as you share in our sufferings, you will also share in the comfort God gives us.* — 2 Corinthians 1:3-7

What Does Grief Look Like during the Holidays?

Grief during the holidays looks much like it does in March or September. The difference is that there are usually not as many public expectations on your time in those "off" months!

* **Difficulty focusing** – Trying to keep track of the tasks and appointments as we move towards a major holiday can be difficult in our normal years. When our thoughts wander to the loss of our loved one or how we are going to make adjustments with the loss of a job or marriage, we look for ways to keep lists and still become frustrated in forgetfulness.

* **Fatigue** – I have heard counselors admonish their patients that grief is hard work and not to be surprised to find themselves unusually tired. Grief is difficult, emotional work which does require more rest which we seldom take, especially around holidays. How often have you come back from visiting relatives at Christmas or Thanksgiving and felt you needed another week off to rest? There may be additional difficulties as you struggle to turn off the constant thoughts and even worries of your mind. Then there is that list-making as you attempt to keep up with all the tasks you have taken on. And don't forget late night board games or early morning fishing expeditions and times of just talking and talking and remembering good times! Any and all of this makes for a tired mind and body.

* **Unexpected tears, sadness** – The Christmas Eve after my son died, I debated right up until the last minute on whether to attend the late night church service. I knew that the music, the candles, the families together and all the memories would probably bring on many tears. I could not decide

if I wanted to bring a pocketful of Kleenex to the service or just skip it altogether.

My two older children stayed home (hundreds of miles away) and had a quiet holiday with their families. That was as it should be and I looked forward to a quiet holiday with my husband. I did not have to fix meals or spend the week before cleaning and decorating the house! But, oh, how lonesome that holiday was!

* **Anger, frustration** – Do not be surprised to feel some anger and frustration that others are going on with their lives, enjoying the holiday with laughter. Yes, that is how it should be! *But* there is some anger at how others go back to their lives while those who have a loss must struggle on. Alone. Life is not fair. *Where* do we channel our anger? *How* do we channel our anger?

It is in the sadness and the anger that we may need some professional help. Whether that is our pastor or a counselor, ignoring these painful emotions will not flush them away. They will become a festering boil. Yes, we may be able to bury them for a period of time but like an infection, without attention it will get worse.

Sometimes we get *stuck* in these emotions. We are angry that this loss has happened to us. We may feel frustrated we did not see it coming and did not prevent the loss. Again, a good counselor can help us to work through and sift through our emotions and bring us out to our new normal.

* **Physical pain, aches** – Every grief book I have ever read and found wisdom in has made the recommendation that 2-3 months after a loss it is a good idea to see your regular physician and have an assessment. Emotional trauma can certainly manifest itself in headaches, nausea, joint and/or back pain, insomnia and other physical symptoms. A physician can often help determine what are transitory problems and what are signs of a serious problem that is not going to go away. Most of us in the medical profession can re-

cite several stories of people who did not pay attention to these symptoms and six months later found themselves diagnosed with life-threatening illnesses.

*   **Worry, guilt** – Here again, a counselor can be very helpful in assisting someone who is traveling the emotional road through grief. It is not surprising to often find ourselves dragging along a sackful of worry about what will the future bring and/or some guilt about what we should have done differently that might have changed the course of events.

    "What's next?" is not a *wrong* question to ask after a major event. How will I find a new job? What is it like to be alone in my house now? How will I raise my children alone?

    Then there's all that guilt about conversations left unsaid or a last conversation was not what we wanted it to be. Maybe we feel that we did not make wise decisions leading up to this life-changing event. We second guess ourselves and think we won't make a good decision again. We need the input of someone with a good perspective of our situation and no agenda but to help us succeed.

During the holidays there are so much is pulling at our attention and keeping us from finding some quiet and time of focus. I believe this is just another reason to reach out to friends, our pastor, or recommended counselor to help us sift through our grief responses to our loss. Do not listen to lies in your mind like:

*   "If you have faith, you won't cry and only know the joy of the LORD."
*   "You and God can do this together. You don't need anyone else."

Jesus wept at the tomb of His friend, Lazarus. Was He weeping because Lazarus died? Probably not since He certainly knew where His friend was headed. But we know Jesus was compassionate toward people, so He might have been weeping in response to the pain that He saw in Mary and Martha. In that short verse of

Scripture, "*Jesus wept*" (John 11:35), it is confirmed to us by God Himself that weeping in grief is okay, even normal.

David wept and fasted at the illness of his son with Bathsheba, even though he had been told by the prophet Samuel that because of his sin this was going to happen. David said that he prayed and fasted in the hope that God would change His mind (2 Samuel 12).

In this fallen world, we have disease, wars, and death. We need each other. We need the comfort of each other to walk the journey of grief; to keep us from rabbit trails and misdirection.

> *As iron sharpens iron, so a friend sharpens a friend.*
> – Proverbs 27:17

AM I GRIEVING? (STILL?)

How long does grief last? How many holidays do I have to get through before this terrible pain stops?

A wise counselor friend once told me that there is an amount of grief we must go through. Sometimes we know that a death is coming. Our loved one is ill or very old. We *anticipate* the loss. We begin grieving as we think about it being "our last Thanksgiving together" or we know there is going to be a layoff or closing of a business and so we *anticipate* how our life will be forever changed because of the loss of the job or an impending divorce.

If the loss is unexpected, then it can take time to get through the shock and *then* begin grieving. And that time of shock can be days, even weeks. And then the grieving comes over us while we are still reeling, beaten up, wore out from all that we have already gone through. It isn't unusual to feel like saying, "No. I just can't deal with this right now!" and emotionally shut down. If we are a friend of this person who is shocked and grieving, we may be concerned about their "shut down." I've been told, however, by professional counselors that it isn't the different phases that people go through or even that they go back to a phase, like numbness, that is of concern. It is when they become "stuck" and can not seem to come out of the emotional numbness that we should get concerned and seek professional help for them.

It would not be unusual to find that holidays continue to bring a new wave of grief two, three, five, even ten years later. Holidays are so grounded in family, in traditions. These memories are difficult to reset into different locations and with changes in the cast of people we expect to be in the familiar scenes. Loss may seem "fresh" when we mourn the loss of the familiarity of those we love.

Allow yourself time in holidays to feel a loss. Be willing to remember what you've loss and also acknowledge what you do have.

A quiet evening looking through photos or sitting quietly on a beach or gazing out over mountains is an excellent setting to bring life into focus and take another step on your journey.

HELP ME GET THROUGH!

The most important thing I can say here is: Do what helps *you*!

Over the years, through the hundreds of families I have listened to and my own experiences in the loss of my parents, my son, a job, a malpractice suit, a divorce and several hurricanes, no one thing got me through all these things. It was my faith *plus* friends and practical, day-to-day options that have brought me to where I am today ... reasonably sane and with my faith in God still attached to me!

Be flexible – yes, that includes canceling your attendance or not holding a dinner or party you may have held *every* year in everyone's memory. *This* year isn't usual. You have a new normal and need time to find what is now going to be normal in your life. As I've said, the first Christmas after my son died, I did not decide to go or not to go to church until the last minute. The following spring, when I received a wedding invitation to his good friend's wedding, I had every intention of going to the wedding. Until the day of the ceremony. I started weeping and I just couldn't stop. I did not want to sit in a wedding and sob! So at the last minute, I did not go.

Make new traditions – A friend puts up an Eternity Tree on her sun porch. It is a Christmas tree with butterfly ornaments. It is her way of remembering those who have died during the year. Butterflies are often used as a symbol for rebirth.

Another friend did a beautiful scrapbook and during the holidays she leaves it out on the coffee table. It is a great way to give visitors permission to bring up "the subject" that is like an elephant in the room which no one wants to acknowledge! In a divorce, this is also a way to acknowledge to your children that you all did have a life with some good memories.

Another family decided to come together for an informal dinner instead of the large midday meal. Instead of multiple entrées, they switched to finger foods. They decided since the time wasn't going to "feel normal," they were going to purposely make the day different.

Let other family members think of options, including the children. If you want some unusual options for new traditions, just ask children and teenagers. They are wonderful about thinking outside the usual box! How about a holiday meal as a picnic? Instead of cooking the whole meal for everyone, tuck away your pride and allow others to bring dishes or host the meal. Most people are more than willing to help but may not be very good at thinking ahead of what is needed.

Ways to remember a loved one at a holiday gathering. I love the LED candles that allow candlelight without the worry of how long the candle will burn. On a side table or the mantle, put a picture of the one who has died with a candle next to the picture. Many families take time during the meal to remember what they are thankful for, whether at Thanksgiving or an end of the year meal. That is also a good time to share some good memories of the one who is now gone.

Do something for someone else. – To remember a loved one or to turn your mind away from your own troubles, doing something for another is a great way to help yourself and someone else. An Angel Tree is a frequent way to help the children in a community to receive clothes, school supplies and toys at Christmas. Putting together Thanksgiving baskets of food is a wonderful way to bless poor families. Remember that they may not have access to regular sized ovens and stoves so cooking may need to be reassessed. During the holidays craft ideas and supplies for children in the hospital or elderly people in long-term care facilities is also a way to remember someone who isn't with you.

Social media – Facebook and websites like *Caring Bridge* (caringbridge.org) provide us with an avenue to share our activities, even our feelings. This can be a way to share with family members and friends who are far away. It should never be seen as the primary way of support if we are grieving. There is a distance inherent in the internet that allows us to project whatever level of coping that we want people to believe. It's a way of saying, "I'm fine!" without actually having someone look into our eyes and see how we really are. Facebook can be a tool but cannot replace a real, live friend!

Opportunities for church support – Many churches have people who are good at reaching out to others who are going through hard times. They like to make a meal and take flowers to shut-ins. Youth groups who visit to sing and bring their own joy and healing are special blessings. People who are grieving need various people to check on them, whether they ask for it or not. A group of youth coming by their home and singing Christmas carols may be the only Christmas carols they hear during the season.

All Saint's Day (November 1) is a time to also remember those who have died in the last year. The celebration can include the reading of names with pictures on posters or digitally projected in slides. Lighting candles, giving simply crafted candles or small potted plants as memorials, allow your heart and imagination develop a way to speak love and support to those who are in need.

Pastors and those who are gifted in visiting and supporting members who are grieving can be very helpful if they create a database of when members or loved ones of members die and then send a card of remembrance at the one year anniversary. Intentionally following up with those who have suffered other losses like their job or a divorce is as important as those who have had a loved one die. It is an important service in the church and needs more than just one person doing it.

FAITH

Faith shows the reality of what we hope for; it is the evidence of things we cannot see.   – Hebrews 11:1

No matter what your beliefs might be, when you are confronted with a great loss, what you do or do not believe, and why you do or do not believe, will force itself to the forefront of your life. If you have never questioned the principles you were taught and accepted as a child, the conflict of what is happening and why it is happening can become the focus of your life.

For two years prior to my 12-year-old son's diagnosis of cancer, I felt an urgency to read my Bible. I read 2-3 chapters a night, wrote notes in the margins, journaled in a notebook, and sat in thought for long periods. And when that day arrived when the doctor said, "Your son has cancer." The scope of my world narrowed down to that one word: Cancer. For the next year, James and I spent our days (and nights) in doctors' offices, laboratories, hospitals and our car, just trying to make it through each day. I could not get my mind to focus down on Bible study. But Scripture passages from the recent past, phrases of things I had written down, those came to me and brought comfort and hope for our future. I was so grateful for the time I had spent in those two years because I could now draw on what I had been taught in the quiet darkness of those nights to bring Light into my life now.

And then there were the people who sent cards, came by to visit or made a quick phone call to let us know they were praying. Most were very helpful. They had no definitive answers but they did have a hug, a touch, a quiet smile that said they were with us.

As a hospice nurse and educator, I have encouraged nurses, social workers, chaplains and volunteers to listen more and speak less. It is a common concern that when we visit and support others, what will we say in response to their questions? How will we explain the "why" of it when we are asking ourselves the same question without an answer?! "I don't know" is an acceptable, truthful answer. The truth is, most people do not expect an answer from us. They are looking for the right, the validation, to ask the question. Giving affirmation that we, too have such questions and are looking to God for answers, tells them they are not alone and in the days and months ahead, we will be with them, studying and asking God for answers.

Time

Will I stop missing you ... in time?
Will I stop seeing you in the distance ... in time?
Will time become more or less meaningful ... in time?
I guess time will tell.

At first time had no meaning. You were not here.
You were there. I wasn't.
Each day was made of endless minutes without you.
Each night a solitude when I listened for your step, your voice.

Then time began to quicken. There were weeks, then months, then years.
And yet you have not aged in my mind's eye.
You still have that stare, with those "old eyes" that know more than they should.
You still have that unexpected laugh, which lights up my world with a joy.

Time has passed. Your friends have married. They have children.
I weep for what could have been, but is not.
I weep for words not spoken,
For possibilities without fruit.

And then, time brings a peace. A smile.
Time will soon mean nothing.
You and I will have more than time.
We will have ... forever.

Books

Black, David Alan. *Running My Race: Reflections on Life, Loss, Aging, and Forty Years of Teaching.* Gonzalez, FL: Energion Publications, 2016. ISBN#: 978-1-63199-294-0.

Hickman, Martha W., *Healing After Loss: Daily Meditations for Working Through Grief.* San Francisco: William Morrow Publishing, 1994. ISBN#: 978-0380773381.

James, John W. and Russell Friedman. *The Grief Recovery Handbook, 20th Anniversary Edition: The Action Program for Moving Beyond Death, Divorce, and Other Losses including Health, Career and Faith.* San Francisco: William Morrow Publishing, 2009. ISBN#: 978-0061686078.

Lewis, C.S. *A Grief Observed.* San Francisco: Harper San Francisco, 2001. ISBN# 978-0060652388.

Neufeld, Jody. *Grief: Finding the Candle of Light.* Gonzalez, FL: Energion Publications, 2007. ISBN# 978-1893729506.

_____. *Daily Devotions of Ordinary People – Extraordinary God.* Gonzalez, FL: Energion Publications, 2004. ISBN#: 978-1893729155.

Noel, Brook and Pamela Blair, PhD. *I Wasn't Ready to Say Goodbye: Surviving, Coping and Healing After the Sudden Death of a Loved One.* Naperville, IL: Sourcebooks, 2008. ISBN#: 978-1402212215.

Roe, Gary. *Please Be Patient, I'm Grieving: How to Care For and Support the Grieving Heart.* Seattle: CreateSpace Independent Publishing, 2016. ISBN#: 978-1530713042.

Westberg, Granger E. *Good Grief: 50th Anniversary Edition.* Minneapolis: Fortress Press, 2010. ISBN#: 978-0800697815.

If You Need a Friend, Give Us a Call

All praise to the God and Father of our Master, Jesus the Messiah! Father of all mercy! God of all healing counsel! He comes alongside us when we go through hard times, and before you know it, he brings us alongside someone else who is going through hard times so that we can be there for that person just as God was there for us. We have plenty of hard times that come from following the Messiah, but no more so than the good times of his healing comfort—we get a full measure of that, too.

When we suffer for Jesus, it works out for your healing and salvation. If we are treated well, given a helping hand and encouraging word, that also works to your benefit, spurring you on, face forward, unflinching. Your hard times are also our hard times. When we see that you're just as willing to endure the hard times as to enjoy the good times, we know you're going to make it, no doubt about it. — 2 Corinthians 1:3-7 (The Message)

Our church is here to be a light in the community; a beacon for individuals and families to find their way home when they feel lost, beaten, and confused. We hope that this booklet has helped you find comfort, healing, and some clarity on the path you are walking.

If we can be of any further help, if you would like to speak to our pastor or a caring member of the congregation, please do not hesitate to give us a call or email us through the information we have given below. We want to share the comfort we have been given with you.

Church name: _____

Contact person: _____

Telephone: _____

Email: _____

Website: _____